MEN'S RIGHTS MANIFESTO OF NEWSOFX.COM

Vivek Singh

Alan Millard

Published by:
Gurucool Publishing
#102, Sai Krupa Nilayam,
Nagendra Nagar, Habsiguda, Hyderabad – 500 007
Ph: 040–69999200,
E-mail: info@gurucoolpublishing.com

Authors: Vivek Singh
Alan Millard

Second Edition – 2021

Scan this QR Code to visit all the links, given in the book:

https://linktr.ee/newsofx

Dedication

I dedicate this book to my mother, father and
sister who instilled in me the ability to know right from
wrong and allowed me to think for myself, inspiring me to
stand against injustice.

*"Life is lived on its own. Other's shoulders are used only at
the time of the funeral."*

Bhagat Singh

Contents

Introduction

The Men's Rights Manifesto of Newsofx.com falls under the premise of equal justice for all, men and women alike, but in which case it is necessary to acknowledge men separately from women due to men being exempt from consideration in acquiring an equal status to women or even considered at all except per negative acknowledgment. This includes blame and rights taken from men. Men's differences from women must weigh in per an equal compromise rather than used to place women above men. Both feminists and traditionalists/chivalrists fail to provide any distinction in support or consideration of men due to extreme female bias and male hatred (misandry), with both (one old, one new) factions being a mere continuance of the past catering to women and demeaning men as disposable pawns for women.

Equal laws, Equal Justice, Equal Rights (Gender Neutral Laws) and Equal Punishment for those Who Misuse Law

One thing that needs to come first to establish a collective of men who will fight legitimately for men's rights and equality to women is abolishing men's conditioned obligation to defend and protect women. This continues to aid misandry and further establishes female-biased laws and precarious conditions for men. Women as equals to men are not entitled to any more protection than are men. Due to conditions created by feminist influence, it is men who are now in more need of protection from women than vice versa.

Given the rising number of false sexual assault allegations against men and their families, and the sculpturing of sex laws to women's subjective and arbitrary discretion, we at Newsofx.com are dedicated to abolishing discriminatory laws created against men and addressing the misuse of laws against men by women. We also seek to protect the identity/reputation of men until proven guilty with stringent punishment for women who file false allegations. Without meeting standard prerequisites, no case is to be filed! We support changing sex laws to reflect a rational compromise between male and female perspectives rather than sex-biased laws subjectively sculptured to the female's arbitrary and sole discretion. Stop using women's sexuality per law to criminalise men through their sexuality!

A Male Stigma of Guilt and Criminality:

What lower status could be applied to a group than one that others rate below them and need protection from? As women are not to be protected any more than are men, men have no more obligation to protect women than woman have to protect men. [This sex-bigotry (misandry) is evident when a man and a woman are having a spat and a man (or even a woman) approaches them and asks the woman if everything is alright.] Protection from what or who? Protection specific to women is not only discriminatory and exclusionary for men but implies a guilty association applied to males as a group. Imagine if this 'protection from' expectation were to be used in reference to any other group of people (e.g. Gays, Blacks, Jews, etc). These are sex-typed stereotypic self-hate obligations built on an accepted prejudice of bad male character. But again due to a lower status assigned to men no one seems to notice that it is men who, especially now, need protection from women.

The female victim card is often played if the sex card or chivalrous card doesn't work. Thus men are pitted against themselves and women are rated as privileged and 'entitled' to protection over men. And either shaming and/or the female's sexuality advantage is often used and thrown into the mix. This takes away men's equal status to women and any equal assessment defining men in their own right—one then defined by women and a servitude to women and a government that blindly serves women. How men relate to women has no application to an exclusive and original male identity. Men defined in their own right have no more obligation to women than vice versa. This is hard for some to accept when men's identity is defined by women. Men are commonly shamed into conformity. But in complement to a man experiencing an existence in his own right, what helps to define a man is a sense of self-worth, accomplishment, and success, for himself, not for others.

Fighting and Exposing Domestic Violence, Misandry, Rape, and Sexual Assault of Boys, Men and Children by Women

We at Newsofx.com support raising awareness of the silenced male victims of domestic violence, misandry, rape and sexual assault. As for abusive partners/mothers, we need to share and spread the word as to why society is not equally concerned about abusive moms? The current narrative only portrays these crimes as a gendered issue, with men as perpetrators and women as victims. Not only is this effort exclusionary of male victims of domestic violence, it is also not supported by evidence—instead driven by raw male hate (misandry). We at Newsofx.com are dedicated to address social, legal, and cultural norms that negatively impact the lives of men and boys. We support the equal treatment of both sexes under the law, primarily focusing on all kinds of violence, to include sexual abuse, rape and physical abuse committed by female offenders against men, other women and children. We debunk the myth that only men commit violence and sex crimes and strive to show that crime has no gender which must be mutually acknowledged and punishable for equal justice to exist.

50-50 Parenting and Equal Physical Custody

As a collective we strive to prevent parent alienation, especially prevalent towards fathers, and bring awareness to this crisis now occurring on a global scale. We address the emotional toll that it brings on parents and children involved due to an unjust court system. Everyday fathers are losing their parental rights and contact with their children due to cultural sex biases that diminish the role and influence of a father and robs children of his love and influence. Fathers are being erased from the family which exclusion is also evident in government programs as WIC (Women, Infants, and Children) and other subsidiary programs that officially exempt fathers from the family. Our mission at Newsofx.com includes bringing men and fathers together as a unified social force, acknowledging the importance of fathers and strengthening the connection fathers have to their children. We support fathers everywhere standing up against the unjust family court system.

Parental Rights are Children's Rights:

Children receive their rights through parental rights. Otherwise, if children are not acknowledged through their parents as minors they belong to the state. We need to also keep in mind that although men and women may have different roles when united, the roles of men and women are equally shared when they separate, especially if children are involved, including custody and support of children, because each parent then takes on the tasks and responsibilities of the other. Roles are split (and of equal importance) pertaining to children and therefore equal physical custody shared by both parents is to be granted as the standard.

Men's Reproductive Rights

Abortion Without Medical Urgency Or the Father's Permission, and Carrying an Embryo to Birth Without the Father's Approval is not Acceptable

We at Newsofx.com support abortion as being a men's rights issue, not merely a women's rights issue and giving fathers an option to "opt" out of being a father with no consequences, the same as a woman can opt out of parenthood via abortion, adoption, or by giving up the child to the other parent, or to having the child if the other potential parent wants it. Men now have absolutely no control over the pregnancy and the impending commitment to parenthood besides preventing it with abstinence or a condom which process is a mutual partner responsibility, and for which both partners are equally accountable. It is not to be a woman's choice against a man's will to force him into fatherhood and financial obligation any more than to force a woman to have sex against her will. (Isn't pregnancy one of the biggest fears a woman has who is raped?) Men currently have no right to denounce parenthood, no right to know his pregnant sex partner is even getting an abortion, no right to a DNA test unless the potential mother gives permission, and men also have no right to be placed on the birth certificate as the father without the mother's consent unless the man is literally MARRIED to her. The mother can put any man's name on the birth certificate and betray the real father, often with neither man having any recourse or right to test the child's DNA, with courts acting as accomplices in this discriminatory and fraudulent process to extort money from men.

Men's reproductive rights are non-existent. Women legally decide if a child be born or aborted without the man's choice in the matter and whether he is enslaved for 18-21 years by her to pay her child support—it's against his will per sex-discriminatory law. He may even be required to pay for a child that is not even his— fraud and extortion enforced by law. And if a man does want a child and a woman does not, he has no legal right to prevent her from aborting it. And his right to have custody is predominantly second to a woman's as is evidenced in most child custody cases. This is not condonable to any rational-minded person or MRA at Newsofx.com.

[Note: As in other cases (e.g. military service and occupational hazards), the government and women consider men to be slaves and disposable for them. Some who interview men claim that those who have gone through custody battles have less legitimate testimonials pertaining to men's rights because they are biased and therefore tainted sources. In my first book I covered the same topic prior to going through my own custody battle, does that mean my own work has less legitimacy now? That's like saying a war veteran who has gone through battle is a biased source of information pertaining to first-hand experience—an actual account. That's who we should gain the information from—the source, one who has actually been there and gone through it.

Some may say that fighting for one's children does not compare to fighting in war, which is just as ridiculous. When a father has his child being taken from him and he can do nothing about it, many fathers would rather fight in battle if it meant having their children and be effective in battle than not being able to fight and lose their children. Is not the reason people go to war is to protect family, especially children? So, don't ever tell any father who's went through court fighting a custody battle for his children that what he says is to be rated less than what someone else has to say who has not had to experience it. What men have to say who have gone through it is worth more rather than less and therefore adds to their credentials as MRAs. The general morale affecting society is directly influenced by this threat much as war affects the morale of a people who experience it, but in this case it is a war being implemented internally. The Post Traumatic Stress symptoms experienced by many war veterans is also experienced by many fathers.]

The Sex Act

The non-acceptability of the sex act and of men's dirty connotation also weighs in heavy with the charge of rape and sexual assault whereas a man's bodily fluids are deemed evil—e.g. Often collected as 'evidence', but evidence of what, the sex act? Sex is not illegal, not bad or wrong, and that is the problem since it is deemed as such concerning men in the sex act, not rape which is exclusively determined at a woman's arbitrary discretion. Imagine if a woman's bodily fluids were used to determine a crime. Just because sex takes place, doesn't mean that a crime takes place. But now with feminist-inspired laws, not holding women equally accountable, basically every heterosexual man is a rapist and every woman is rated as a child given the ability to subjectively declare a felony crime at her arbitrary and sole discretion. A man has no such oppressive power over a woman at his discretion with a lack of equal accountability.

Applying to the dirty/guilty stigma attached to the male's sexuality, something many of us have heard is "A penis has no conscience." This is ridiculous. Does a vagina have a 'conscience'? A penis is a mere body sex organ as a vagina which has no more or less of a conscience than a penis. This is as silly as assigning the same assessment to the mouth when one is hungry for food. Wouldn't the assessment be more accurately applied to the female who sexually teases the male?

The reference of 'cute' to something sexy a woman wears (dress, swimming suit) is paradoxical. There is nothing cute about something that is sexy. Cute is for puppies, babies, and children. Cute applied to sex inaccurately pairs up with innocence, lack of accountability and not being equally culpable. The term 'cute' is merely a cover-up excuse for female sexual culpability in dress and her lack of accountability for it.

Males are deemed 'Dirty' and less Innocent at birth:

"When does a child's sexuality become 'dirty'? Shortly after being born? Is it not in the eyes of the beholder? With sex looked upon as dirty and shameful (often the case with religion and its very strict guidelines), the sex with the higher sex-drive (male) is deemed dirtier than the other (female). But there is more to it in comparison than this. The chivalry better-than-you female factor weighs in." And this applies to the issue of male circumcision.

My Body My Rules, Circumcision, Male Genital Mutilation (MGM)

Every year thousands of baby boys are subjected to circumcision—Male Genital Mutilation (MGM). Moments after boys are born most are scarred for life by this primitive and barbaric religious-based practice. Due to the male's sexuality being 'dirty' the male is the only one of the two sexes routinely circumcised in western society. Circumcision carried out unnecessarily on boys can cause them to have many problems in childhood and later in life. These include psychological issues, sexual health problems, panic attacks, erectile dysfunction, infection, loss of tissue that adds sensation to the penis, and, in some extreme cases, even death to the male infant.

The foreskin adds sensation to the most sensitive part of the penis, and removal of it results in far less enjoyable sexual stimulation. As one source conveys, the foreskin is a normal, protective, functioning organ and the practice began in the 1800s to prevent masturbation. Refer to National Organization of

Circumcision Information Resource Centers at www.nocirc.org. Male intimacy can not help but be negatively affected by circumcision, with a protective sheath providing lubricant and millions of nerves (sensory receptors) removed. An insightful source also conveys, "Nature does not make mistakes, especially not with the reproductive organs. Humans have evolved over millions of years, and in the struggle for survival, any body part that was not doing a useful job would have disappeared or been modified (Church and State: Challenging religious privilege in public life, retrieved from www.churchandstate.org.uk/2012/11/the-foreskin-and-the-origins-of-circumcision/). Due to our sexuality being considered "dirty or impure," circumcision has been used as a way to "purify" someone (History of Circumcision, retrieved from www.cirp.org/library/history/). And this is why the practice is only performed on males (baby boys) in our society.We live in modern societies where the genitals of baby girls are rightly protected under specific laws but not those of boys. Circumcision is a form of genital mutilation that should be illegal. We at Newsofx.com support no excuses for such primitive and barbaric religious and cultural practices and believe that baby boys are to have the same basic human rights as baby girls. For this reason we oppose all forms of genital mutilation.

Sexual Chivalry:

Other disregard for the male's sexuality, and what may be accurately referenced as chivalry applied to human sexuality, is when the male's sexuality is deemed inadequate to serve the female's. This is evident in the diagnostic terms specifically applied to men as 'pre-mature' ejaculation—a condition that does not exist when a man is alone and masturbates. Thus the term is only derived from using the female's sexuality as the standard when a man and woman are together. The same sex-biased assessment often applies to impotency which is often due to the woman not having the sexual attributes that are necessary to sexually stimulate the man. Like in most other aspects of society the male is held accountable for the female and something is deemed wrong with him if he differs from her. As per the term cited above, nature does not make mistakes, especially applying to our sexuality. The sooner a man ejaculates, the sooner, per biology, he is assured of reproducing. And due to the male having more of a need for sex, it is his sexuality that, if anything, should set the standard.

Chivalry is Misandry

Chivalry has been conveyed by some to mean being courteous and polite, akin to the Golden Rule. But falling short of *doing unto others as you would want them to do unto you*, it contains the female discriminatory flaw of treating women better than men. Being chivalrous is 'polite' just like a black person being pressured to give up his seat for a white person is 'polite'. Sometimes said in reference to its expression is "Chivalry is not dead," just as one could say discrimination against blacks is not dead. It can not be denied that in either case one is privileged at the expense and burden of someone else. Chivalry no less expresses the hatred of men than racial prejudice and discrimination expresses the hatred of a race. For justice and equality to live chivalry must die. Chivalry's common usage and application expresses favoritism and preferential treatment towards women and is a practice bound by a female entitlement status that preceded the women's movement. The following source accurately regards chivalry as male hatred (misandry) and conveys an effort by a woman, Agnes McHugh, who in 1917 crusaded against chivalry on men's behalf—an effort spurred by many women getting away with killing their husbands: Agnes McHugh's Crusade Against Chivalry – 1917. Retrieved from http://www.avoiceformen.com/series/unknown-history-of-misandry/agnes-mchughs-crusade-against-chivalry-1917/. A comprehensive explanation of chivalry, its origination, and how feminism is built upon it, is also offered through the following source: Chivalry, 2015 at https://reference.avoiceformen.com/wiki/Chivalry. One source refers to the female entitlement status and preferential treatment of women as feminisation within cultural tradition (Hall, 2012). Chivalry as a prerequisite to feminism gave women a higher standing over men that allowed women to acquire even more under the guise of women's liberation. Chivalry has resulted in discriminatory behaviour, policies, and laws (VAWA is one example, Title IX is another amongst many more), defying the ethical standards and premise of equal justice for all supposedly secured by our U. S. Constitution.

Chivalry's female-biased prerequisite to feminism not only provides a foundation for feminism but continues to be of use providing women what they want at the expense of men who are groomed from boyhood to serve women and thereafter continually conditioned to cater to women's demands—politically, economically, socially, dating, marriage and thereafter in divorce and child custody. The modern expression "Happy wife, happy life" sums it up. In other words, you make your wife happy or, as a threat, you will have hell to pay for it—sort of a concession for feminism's acceptance of marriage but also applying after in alimony and child support payments.

Chivalry and being a "Gentleman":

The term and practice of being a 'gentleman' is synonymous with chivalry/female superiority bias, serving women and placing women above men (on a pedestal) as royalty status—e.g. A man stands when a woman enters a room, a woman goes first (Ladies first) as he opens the door for her when she does as he serves her in every way, offering his seat and standing while she sits. Gentleman is the individual assignment of this female bias (chivalry) and akin to the status of black slaves prior to getting their freedom—misandry in its purest form. 'Gentleman' is a term often used to shame men into conformity—"You sir are no gentleman." But this serves as a compliment to any self-respecting man—"You ma'am are no lady to expect it."

A man is to show no more regard than is equally expressed by a woman (reciprocal) regarding men for him to qualify as a gentleman. This otherwise establishes that a man is not good enough (an 'equal') to a woman unless he compensates by doing more for her than she does for him to 'make up' for his inferior status discrepancy. Due to the self-hate definition and servitude contingency regarding one who is supposed to be an equal, no self-respecting man or genuine men's rights advocate qualifies as a gentleman. Indeed, nothing is equal in this degraded status assigned to men. Gentleman is an assigned title to keep men oppressed and chained to the male servitude/chivalry status that has kept men oppressed for centuries. Being a lady does not require any sacrifice via servitude or risk of her life for a man nor openly express her inferior status to him. Being a gentleman is to have no more qualifiers catering to the opposite sex than does being a lady in public or otherwise. The discriminatory and and self-hating practice of chivalry has contaminated the political environment and laws as well as the social scene and male/female arrangements from mating through marriage, divorce, alimony, child support, and child custody.

Newsofx.com stresses awareness as to how social/cultural influences carry some form of misandry and/or suppress an unabated status for men's equality. Religion, feminism, culture, and tradition all weigh in at varying degrees to prevent a free realm of expression regarding men's rights/equality and allowing men to be defined in their own right which includes an equal self-worth and value assigned to men as to women.

But men are often their own worse enemies too. As they have been groomed to stand against other men, they have yet to form a meaningful collective to stand up to women as women collectively stand up to men. What lies in the way of men's equality most is the hate of men by other men.

Establishing in Men an Equal self-worth to Women

Men are groomed from boyhood to hate themselves and serve women. They continue to be conditioned to serve women at their own expense throughout their lives. As part of their conditioning men are forbidden from giving regard to themselves and are demeaned and shamed for doing so due to a degraded identity assigned to them—one of servitude, use, and disposability. With an assigned lower status, the male is groomed to prove himself. This continues from boyhood on through manhood, with women assigned as the judges to his performance. The degraded male status directly applies to the next category.

The Social Scene:

The social/mating scene commonly attests to an unequal status attributed to men compared to women in which case the burden is selfishly and discriminately placed on men to initiate contact. (Female egotism reveals that women commonly think they are 'above' asking men out or paying their way. These women are not worth having anyway.)

Not only revealing and expressing a lower status assigned to men, this sexist and selfish expectation/practice conveniently and hypocritically sets men up, not only to include rejection but now subjects a man in this degraded role to a multitude of charges all sculptured to the female's arbitrary and subjective discretion. Newsofx.com stands that no self-respecting man accepts this role nor does any decent woman who equally regards a man place it upon him. Prior to feminists taking over the equality effort, when it began to equally consider men, and even in the past to a limited extent with 'ladies choice' dances and other social events in which case women responsibly expressed their interest, women (who desired men at all) took on more accountability in the mating process, especially for what they did and choices they made, which included the sex act and sexual interactions. *Just like a friendship, a relationship is a mutual responsibility due to being an equal arrangement in which two people are engaged, and it is therefore a mutual responsibility between the two individuals to initiate one. Women often fail to do their part and, worse, are hypocritically even critical of the men who do theirs, with laws accommodating this egotistical female hypocrisy.*

A Relationship should rate at par with a Friendship:

Why can't men and women just meet as friends as they do with the same sex? Friends don't place unequal expectations on each other or try to use each other unless they are unworthy as friends, which characteristic should make them equally unworthy as potential mates. A man should therefore not be held any more responsible than a woman when on a date ("I want her home by..."). If she is old enough to date, then a woman is old enough to be responsible for herself just as much as her male counterpart. When making friends, one friend isn't held more responsible than the other. Should not dating be held to the same standard as friendship? (Why call them boy or girl -friends unless that is exactly what they are—friends?) [A very revealing correlation is that laws are somehow not needed for friendships yet they are needed for mating.] Thus, a man should not have to sacrifice his self-respect or be held more accountable to be with a woman than vice versa. A woman is supposed to be his equal.

The pair-bonding process is worthless unless both parties express mutual effort and interest. A relationship resulting built upon any other premise is lacking as well. (e.g. Again, as it applies, the *Happy wife, happy life* expression indicates an extremely imbalanced and selfish arrangement.) A flawed foundation results from a one-sided arrangement of demeaned status, servitude and debt starting from the mating process through marriage and after in divorce, alimony, and child custody—politically and legally, all sculptured to women's favor at men's expense. The most telling of an unequal male status and non-mutual arrangement is the social scene and mating/dating process arrangement.

Expressed initial interest, mutual desire, effort and expense in the social scene is a must to establish a basic premise of equality for men and women. A man is not to be given or to accept any lower status that makes him less sought and more susceptible to rejection than a woman. As endorsed by Newsofx.com, this is not acceptable under equality guidelines or mere equal regard as a human being. Again, a relationship is a mutual adult responsibility, so a woman is equally responsible for putting mutual effort into forming one. This includes equal initiation and mutual offerings of gifts etc.. so as not to give the woman any more value/status than the man. The wedding ceremony too will therefore need to accommodate by denouncing any more special value and attention provided to the bride over the groom. Any other arrangement is unequal and merely based on a status arrangement that traditionally applies to men as inferior to women. Again, friendships are not created this way. And don't women make friends with other women? Should a standard rating below friendship apply to the mating/social scene and pair-bonding process? This reveals no worthwhile quality as a friend just as it reveals no worthwhile quality as a mate.

In-the-know people and intellectuals need to come together to form a more advanced collective pertaining to men's rights to create a true equality standard. Many are instead led astray, even accepting concepts that are in contrast to men's rights due to common social rituals and ways that haunt us from the past, often through religion, culture, and tradition. This is in addition to feminism's influence that has added opposition and more misandry to the mix.

Those with any conscience or good will toward men will not merely place men back in the yoke of serving women and the government as disposable pawns and servants. Instead they will advocate for men to have an identity in their own right rather than one dictated by women and the government—basic ownership and slavery attached to a predetermined and defined 'manhood'.

Any sex differences as sex-drive (e.g. men's greater need for sex), without negative judgement, will also be granted full respect, recognition and consideration in mutual compromise to women. Human sexuality is still looked upon as naughty and dirty. Most adults are still children mentally when it comes to sex. However, such ignorance and taboo leads to major problems and discrepancies, with misandric laws sculptured from such ignorance and prejudice. As sex is looked down upon as dirty, those who need it most (men) are also seen as dirty, and those who are the providers of that need (women) have a tremendous advantage. The female's sexuality is seen as more 'innocent' and therefore men with their sexual needs are deemed more guilty/dirty than are women. This stigma does wonders to grant exclusive power to women and how they can use that power against men.

[Note: Why do we continue to place traditional expectations on men but not on women, especially now since those resources previously available for men to fulfil those expectations have been split with women, and especially when men enacting their part in the mating process are demonised and set up to charges due to newly implemented laws that specifically target men? Men's biologically-derived counterpart value to women's is providing sustenance, which has now been tapped by women via EEO and it (per a conversion to government currency) is the male's only exchange value to which *the oldest profession* (prostitution) attests.]

Worse, men are set-up perfectly when the female's sexuality can be weaponised and used maliciously against them. (If any comparable power over women were exclusively held by men, restrictions would have been imposed long ago—the acquisition of money or sustenance being the closest male equivalent which has been provided by law to women and directly accessed by women). Women marched in the streets decades ago chanting they would use their sexuality against men, as their exclusive power would allow them to do so. With women lacking equal accountability to men, few restrictions have been placed on women's sexuality, and those that have existed were lifted under the title of sexual liberation which came at men's further sexual oppression and persecution via new laws created that exempt women from mutual accountability (e.g. alcohol consumption when engaged in sex considered rape of her, regret sex deemed rape after the fact, and that she can even change her mind once engaged in the act, which are actually violations of the male with whom she is engaged) for their sexuality much as children rather than adults—the equivalent to children with guns due to the felony charges at their arbitrary discretion and dire consequences subjectively wielded by them. (This is extreme abuse of power.) Rape only occurs given the desire of a woman with a man at her mercy/sole discretion. No other crime is so subjective and arbitrarily defined at only one person's sole discretion. This has got to change by incorporating the male's perspective per his needs, mutual consideration, and equal rights. Sexual stimulation is instigated by visual means on the female's behalf. This is self-evident through lingerie and pornography—well-known and used by women on a daily basis, yet dishonestly is not admitted. The female often initiates sex this way, which if not sincere or is unwanted, is to be held against her. Laws are so hypocritical that the man who enacts his part in the sexual process in kind is the one blamed instead.

[Prostitution only occurs because women are those who charge for sex, yet newly implemented prostitution laws hold men accountable.]

Tradition and religion weigh heavily against men in many other ways to include harboring chivalry which also weighs in on the brevity of the sex act and indiscriminately supports any proposed sexual violation exclusively determined by women and chivalrous men. And due to this female 'victim/innocent' status acknowledgment of men's sexual abuse by women is voided. Women can, and do, get away with the abuse of men since men are supposed to *take it* (abuse) *like a man* and since they are deemed more dirty, bad, and of a lower calibre and disposable status to women.

Female Privilege and Sexist Expectations:

Could we not accurately say that modern-day women are spoiled? Have you ever tried reasoning with a spoiled child? Just as spoiled children, the majority of today's women can not be reasoned with. (This is because the acceptance of reason would void their privileges.) Men are left with no bargaining tools or ability because women have been given everything, even access to the source of men's provisions. For men and women to have equal status, women will need to give up much of what they now have. Doubtful women are willing to do this, in which case fair laws and social standards will have to be implemented against women's will. But this clashes with society's obsession with striving to please women. (e.g. Anything against a woman's will is made illegal.)

Not all Misandrists are Women:

Let's not forget that not all man-haters are feminists or women. Men groomed to serve women from boyhood and hating other males are a major problem too. Revealing the likeness in feminism's older sister chivalry, traditional women had many of the same male-hate sentiments too, considers men's existence to merely be of service to women.

Once men paved the way for women by their expense and use they were no longer needed and feminism took over. Men were then conveniently hated and condemned since their existence no longer provided any use to women. But men should not have this use/disposable identity to begin with but instead one assigned that acknowledges men as human beings needing to have their own identity defined in their own right rather than women's. Comparatively little psychology exists that pertains specifically to men or that defines men in their own right. Given their pedestal status and that men must strive to please them, women are often granted authority as 'psychologists', occurring even in the past (e.g. Ann Landers, Dear Abby), and often drag their boyfriends or husbands into a counsellor to merely 'prove' they are right if their boyfriends/husbands dare oppose their wishes or disagree with them. With our educational system, especially psychology and the social sciences, contaminated by feminists, a man is subject to extreme mental abuse who succumbs to this type of mental 'treatment'. This social condition is likely a major contribution to male suicide.

As a form of abuse and domestic violence, nagging and hen-pecking are well-known terms applying to female abuse of men, yet this is not even a crime as it would be if it were a well-known traditional abuse of women. It has even been conveyed as humorous or demeaning to the male victim who is subjected to it.

Preserving Accurate References, Academic and Historic Integrity

Prior to the early 1900s time-period the word feminism did not even exist. But when it did first occur in reference form, feminism meant to feminize, make feminine, which makes more sense because the masculine counterpart in the term (root word) is otherwise not represented for the term to legitimately stand for equality of both sexes or an equal balance between masculine and feminine. When later identified as a cause feminism was also defined as a cult.

Feminist 'scholars' (an oxymoron if there ever was one) are now changing our references to 'correct' the past to their preference, even referring to different "waves" of feminism. Save all old references since they bear evidence to the truth.

Newsofx.com does not endorse the new idea of granting feminism any so-called 'waves' and contaminating historical documentation with this inaccuracy for feminism to 'justify' itself as legit. Accurate historical record is not conducive to allowing feminism to establish some sort of credit that is not only unwarranted but that does not even exist in the past. This self-promotion is even fraudulently applied to prominent women of the past who did not identify as feminists and some who were advid non-feminists. To deem prominent women of the past as feminists merely because they were women is no different than to attach the identity of Nazi just because someone happens to be German.

The female for male resources trade-off exchange is a basic human dynamic that goes unheeded in determining sociological conditions

Lack of Human male/female Unification: Money and Misandry:

Misandry was thrown into the mix correlating to the time EEO/AA was implemented by the government. One might therefore question, all other things being equal, if without the male hatred introduced by feminists whether women would equally desire men given they now have money. More research, along with approval and funding for that research, is needed to confirm the consequential impact each has had on society. Male hatred and access to male biologically-derived resources via government assistance and/or equal employment opportunity have bought women off. (Could a form of population control be responsible for orchestrating this result?)

A contradiction dictated by sociological terms affecting human dynamics is that when women receive money from other sources besides men, they have less desire for men. [But the female's new role came with a hatred of men, and that also weighs in too.] The same could be said for men and sex. When sex is available to men outside of marriage as through prostitution, men do not desire women, especially if packaged with hate and selfish expectations. Equal employment opportunity and government assistance is to women what prostitution is to men, but one (women taking men's jobs) is forced against men and the other (prostitution) is illegal for men. Money (government currency) is the government's liquidation of male assets biologically-derived from male sustenance provision. Feminists took something totally out of bio-sociological context (and from a biological derivative) and claimed women were cheated. But women cheated themselves and society by implementing laws that contradicted a human biological premise and yet failed to follow through in all other aspects of human existence to which this role applies to men.

The male biologically-derived sustenance united men and women in a complementary social order. This resource has now been used to do exactly the opposite per government coercion via EEO/AA (Equal Employment Opportunity/Affirmative Action) combined with the hate propaganda (that women had been cheated) packaged with it. Ironically, women only desire those men who are still allowed access to their male-derived resources. And yet still women complain about men as a collective earning more than women! Wouldn't this be like men complaining about not accessing sex even after it was deemed illegal to deny equal sexual opportunity to men? Very much so, if we are speaking openly and honestly about human dynamics.

Prostate Cancer

We at Newsofx.com support helping men survive prostate cancer and promote men enjoying a better quality of life. We strongly advocate funding research to find causes and treatments, raising the profile of the disease and improving care for its victims. We believe that men are to receive equal regard and financial support for their diseases and illnesses.

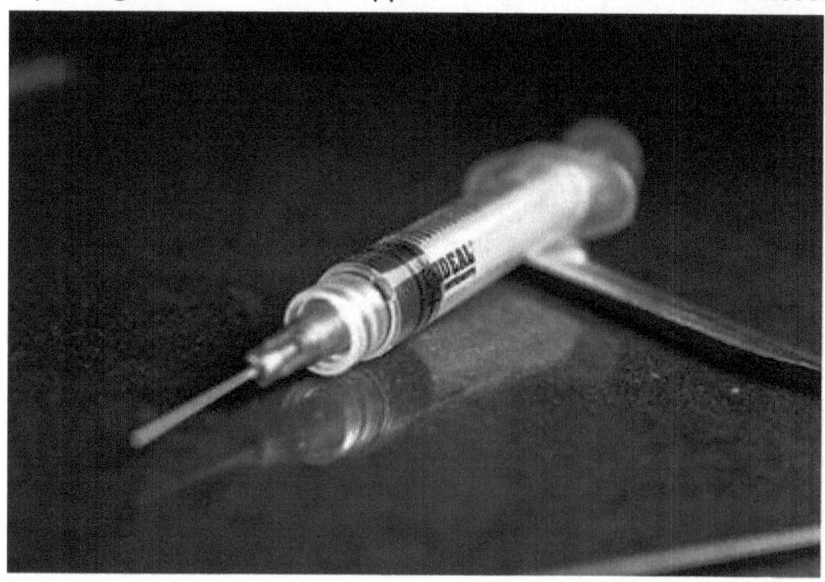

About 1 man in 8 will be diagnosed with prostate cancer during his lifetime. Prostate cancer is the most commonly diagnosed cancer among men in the U.S. excluding certain skin cancers. There is a misconception about prostate cancer that it isn't fatal when in fact it is the second leading cause of cancer death in American men, behind only lung cancer. Prostate cancer is the second most commonly occurring cancer in men and the fourth most commonly occurring cancer overall. There were 1.3 million new cases in 2018.

While it is true that prostate cancer is largely curable if diagnosed and treated early, patients with advanced prostate cancer have a less favorable prognosis. Advanced prostate cancer is defined as cancer spreading beyond the original tumor.

Male hormones such as testosterone, otherwise important for male health, cause prostate cancer to grow and survive. Early treatments for prostate cancer attempt to lower levels of testosterone level in the body. This is known as a form of hormone therapy.

However, prostate cancer tumors may actually begin to grow again even if the level of testosterone level in the body is low. At this point the cancer is also considered to be advanced.

Researchers are studying why this occurs in their attempts to better understand how to develop treatment for prostate cancers.

Guadeloupe had the highest rate of prostate cancer in 2018, followed by Martinique.

Supporting Positive Masculinity

Many reap the benefits of men and their masculine attributes yet condemn masculinity without giving men due credit for their accomplishments or acknowledging that men are good. For every male criminal there are thousands of good men. As for men's equality, we must first realize that men and women can't replace each other. As creatures of mother earth and God, both sexes are designed to complement one another and must exist in their own right which includes an equal value and status to each other. Everything men do can't be done as well by women and much of what women do can't be done as well by men. Men and women are equal but different—opposites that support each other. Men's role in advancing society through technology applying to labor and agriculture, the military, mining, and occupations as a firefighter, police officer, etc. have been cherished. We use and depend on these professions and advancements everyday, yet we still condemn the source of their creation with no credit? Through the creation of a constitution, government, and just laws, along with technology, men and masculinity advanced society. It's not masculinity that is toxic, it's the lack of a positive version that is the problem—one that must be designed in men's own right instead of one designed as a mere disposable servitude to women and the government. Bad men don't become good when they stop being men, they become good when a positive masculinity is developed from childhood. And this includes one not designed by women that is often turned on men.

A Healthy form of Masculinity is one that can not be turned against itself. It can not be subjectively defined by women nor men who are influenced by women. Masculinity is to be defined in men's own right which acknowledges, considers, accepts, and respects basic male needs and characteristics. Men must treat other men equal to how they treat women in a healthy form of masculinity. Due to what's apparently a modern-day insecurity men have gone to the extreme in their expression of 'masculinity'. The movie title *The Expendables* identifies the extreme effect of a toxic or negative masculinity differing even from the past—e.g. The days of *Father Knows Best* and Jack Lalanne. At the same time a barbaric masculinity is being promoted we are denouncing bullying and acknowledging men's feelings, with a personal and individual value attributed as being equal in value to a woman's. Any worthy masculine identity can not be turned on itself. It's devoid of self-hate. Being a kind, good person equally applies in character identity to a man as well as to a woman. Equal expectations of qualification determining the status of a good person (and its expression) applies equally to both sexes. If we had common decency expressed by men (and women) equally applied toward men that considered violence toward men just as unacceptable as toward women we would then have an expression of equality of the sexes—thus *equal justice for all*.

Think about the effect for a moment. Who's going to be available to be pitted against each other when men (and women) are groomed to be just as considerate of men as they are women? Governments and women will no longer have human pawns at their disposal. They would have to resolve their differences without the use of others to fight their battles. Once leaders realize they would have to be the first to sacrifice their lives to settle their differences, they would likely find better, nonviolent ways to resolve them.

Image Means nothing without Content and Substance:

Are not men's rights to men more important than their masculine image? How masculine is it to have no status as men, to be second-class citizens as men? There's little dignity or pride to be had from a gutted 'masculinity'. Masculinity becomes nothing but a face, a facade—something without substance—if not supported by rights, including the right for men to exist in their own right. This existence otherwise fits the masochistic male identity that has been used to define 'masculinity. Is it possible to have a lesser identity than ever before yet still be masculine? Sure, but only if we define masculinity as a mere servitude to others and self-loathing. There is no regard for men in a servitude and disposable role. Take it *'like a man'* about sizes up his existence without thought or consideration given to a man as a real person. This idea of masculinity without a priority given to men's equal rights depletes any worthy masculine/male status and serves well to undermine men's basic human rights.

Are men only capable of having 'equal' rights if women allow it? Apparently needing female approval, many MRAs are so grateful that women are involved supporting men's rights that they place them in a recognized status above seasoned male MRAs. This seems to be a strong indicator of a sociological paradox and potential historical repeat, providing an example of how men must still gain women's approval to acquire what they are equally entitled to have in their own right. But under this contingency arrangement, how will it be acquired in their own right and not again in women's? (This is evidence of a self-perpetuating matriarchy.)

An interesting point is that women to have what they want don't seek men's approval. To have legitimacy should men not acquire what they want on their own too? To be legit, and have an existence defined in their own right, they will. Otherwise, men's existence will again be earmarked by women's approval not unlike chivalry and female bias (feminist) guidelines.

What defines a man in his own right? Accomplishments? Much more than that? Somethings may have yet to be discovered. A personal design, if a man's allowed one, may include content that we may not realize are vital to men, not defined as masculine but not necessarily feminine either but male nevertheless.

In Summation:

Men must quit hating themselves and come to rational terms first before they can expect to get anywhere with implementing real equality standards. This includes men having an existence in their own right instead of women's and the government's with a mere pawn identity defining who they are.

Military Service

Men and women are to be equally obligated to serving in the military with both required to register for the draft. Qualification standards and abilities will determine who is qualified for what positions within—the best fit.

A Male Identity and Self-value appropriated to Match:

Men being disposable and whose existence is only to serve others, women, and the government are often shamed for having any exclusive needs (wanting equal rights to women)—in fact rated as disgusting and selfish. Religion, tradition, and feminism all do this. Along the same lines is use of the term 'male ego' since all ego belongs to women. Again, males being 'proudly disposable', compared to women, are not supposed to have any ego—mere personal value and self-respect as males in their own right. This degraded status is often applied to men risking rejection, taking physical and mental abuse, all included in performing a very disadvantaged and sex-degraded role assigned to them.

Equal Pay for Equal Work

We at <u>Newsofx.com</u> basically support equal pay for equal work and responsibilities. If a woman does the same work and assumes the same level of responsibily as a man she should receive equal payment, but along with this role comes increased social responsibility and accountability such as accepting men as mates with a lower income, women therefore paying on dates, etc.. Manhood and a criteria for a male as a mate can therefore no longer include his financial status nor expectations, otherwise women are hypocrites.

Newsofx.com supports equal pay for equal work but if only when women do the same job as men do and when they accept societal responsibilities that come with it. Not to stereotype, but generally speaking, fewer women than men are in senior management positions. If women are in occupations as primary school teachers, secretaries, or a healthcare worker, which are lower paid positions, they can't expect to receive a higher pay attributed to positions in these fields that require more expertise, education, liability, and accountability. That would not be true equality. That would be **Unequal Pay for Unequal Work** (and thus female entitlement) which is not what <u>newsofx.com</u> endorses. Newsofx.com supports women acquiring a higher education level (along with the training, experience, and expertise) that allows them to competently occupy higher positions, as well as their commitment to get more hours worked per week to match their desire to receive more financial compensation. In other words, they need to earn it the same as men do. Newsofx.com also supports the idea that women enter male dominated jobs to get a true sense of equality, like entering occupations as the law enforcement or military, or becoming a miner, sewer worker, firefighter etc. to get a real sense of equity applying to income and earning it as do men.

Newsofx.com supports women competing with men in availability, hours of work performed, quality of job, etc. to get equal pay as a true sense of equality (or that is equity) applied to income. However, women are to also meet the same qualification standards as to be equally competent to men in the professions and those served. Newsofx.com supports women's maternity leave but also endorses maternity leave for single dads and fathers who are also working to support these pregnant women through their post pregnancy and childbirth experience.

In addition, if women are to be paid the same as men for the same work as men, they also assume a social responsibility to use that same money to equally contribute to the union of men and women in which case they approach, ask out men and provide for men and the family as did men for women in the past when they possessed those same assets. Jobs and occupations and the financial resources secured originated through men by nature. This human dynamic must be further examined in application to women's equal employment opportunity and in how that affects society and men's personal needs that used to be fulfilled by them acquiring their assets they exchanged for women's. A tremendous imbalance has now occurred that works to tear apart our society, especially combined with misandry. Money in the hands of men ensures a better result for both men and women and the perpetuation of family and society. The sad fact is that when women earn their money it is spent more on themselves than on men or the family.

Women now drive the world economy.
How Women's Economic Power Is Reshaping The Consumer

Market.
Statistics on the Purchasing Power of Women.
20 Facts And Figures To Know When Marketing To Women.

39

Equal Employment Opportunity reduced wages to enslave Two for the price of one. Putting women in the workforce and splitting wages with men works well to boast the profits of big business and taxation by the government, making it necessary thereafter for both men and women to be enslaved. And keeping with this status quo arrangement will require that a negative rapport continues to exist between men and women. Equal Employment Opportunity not only reduced wages to enslave two workers for the price of one, but redirected the resources that in the past provided sustenance to perpetuate humanity (people & their progeny) that is now contributing to government and big business instead.

The Sex Gestapo, Created by Anti-male Propaganda via Emotional Appeal

The National Sex Offender List was mandated by President Clinton in 1996 in response to the tragic fate of 8-year-old Megan Kanka in 1994 who was raped and killed. This was a terrible occurrence, of course, but not something that should be used (emotionally exploited) to change our basic laws. This case did not involve a law-abiding type of individual and is an extreme exception from the majority of cases, involving a child and her murder. Furthermore, instead of being irrationally influenced by emotion, it is necessary that we acknowledge that an act as this was considered just as terrible in the past too, prior to creating more sex laws as this one. (This is a key point applying to many modern-day laws that act to take away our freedomthrough mere emotional exploitation.) Law-makers, per a feminist mindset, used this event, and an emotionally-charged climate resulting, as an excuse to brand everyone found guilty of any sex crime by creating a list of all offenders, to include sex acts (and even non-sexual acts) not even relevant to such a case. There exists no separate list of people who have committed other crimes. Were not Jews segregated in a similar fashion when a popular anti-Semitic climate was created?

This is an easy avenue to effect a dictatorship-type of government control. This list of condemnation amounts to branding people, even after their sentences have been served. The Nazi-type procedure (and a protocol supporting it) has never before existed in our country nor has it been implemented upon our people which relentless persecution is a violation of our freedom and liberties, including rights to privacy. (Once the sentence has been served, the price is paid.)

In many cases pedophiles are something we create, and often it's through The 'Dirty Seed' of Maleness:

An incident took place on a Florida beach where a man and a woman had sex and a child witnessed it. The man was sentenced to two and a half years in prison and the woman was sentenced to a short time in jail (which had already been served by the time of sentencing), but both had to register as sex offenders. How can two people be mutually engaged in a legal sex act (both preoccupied with each other), yet at the same time be involved in an illegal act with someone else, with the man punished more for it than his female partner? Refer to Florida man caught having sex on a beach gets two and a have years in jail at http://www.theguardian.com/us-news/2015/jul/06/florida-man-sex-beach-convicted-prison. This man wasn't having sex with himself. Blame specifically targeted him for performing his part in the sex act per a video played at the trial—"showed Alvarez moving on top of Caballero in a sexual manner in broad daylight" (Couple found guilty of having sex on Florida beach, forced to register as sex offenders. May 4, 2015. Miami Herald. Retrieved from http://www.miamiherald.com/news/state/florida/article201 91164.html). Read the input by the people who responded to this nonsense. This is sex-biased discrimination for a law that shouldn't exist in the first place. (Indecent exposure may apply perhaps but nothing more. They weren't harming anyone.) And besides, would not the child's parent share some of the blame? If this sexual exposure is considered "dangerous," isn't it the parent's responsibility to keep the child out of 'harm's' way? If the child fell over a cliff, would that not be more harmfull? (Wouldn't the same 'violation' apply to a kid on the farm who witnesses farm animals having sex? Maybe the kid could learn something.) Again, sex is not bad and is itself not illegal. Besides not be imprisoned, the couple should certainly not have to register as sex offenders because that is not what took place. This mindset, and a law that comes with it, is not only a threat to the freedom of others but mere subjective condemnation for life via our sexuality. What if a nude male statue has a penis depicted? Does this mean the statue sexually violates children who see that? If a child inadvertently sees a movie that shows a man's penis, is someone then a sex offender too? And would the parent gaurdian not then be accountable for it? This terrible law has got to go, with people charged compensated and cleared of any charges, especially that brand one a condemned sex offender.

[Note: The female's body is considered 'sacred' whereas the male's is 'disgusting,' with the male's sexual body parts now reduced in reference to "junk" by both men, lacking self-respect, and by women who disrespect men. His junk contrasts with a past reference of his *family jewels.* Imagine referring to the female's sexual body parts as her junk. Due to its degraded status, the male's, not the female's, sexuality is used to determine indecency. Women go practically nude without ridicule and, as we've covered, sex laws accommodate this discrimination. (It's ridiculous and inexcusable that if a child sees an adult male's privates, rather than mere indecent exposure, it's now a sex crime against a child.) Let's be big enough people to accept and respect the male's sexuality as we do the female's.]

Our forefathers, through the test of time, would have never sacrificed the basic laws we have due to emotions that surround certain issues, incidents, and events. The same emotional antics are used to change gun laws. If our forefathers had given into their emotions, our rights, that include equal justice for all, would have been sacrificed long ago. Lynchings are an example of the same emotionally-based actions and matching mentality. Our nation's laws and people's rights and liberties are too sacred to be subject to mere emotional influence and an irresponsible populous so easily swayed to change laws due to certain incidents that occur. When we allow emotion to change basic laws we undermine justice, especially as in this case, with modern-day sex laws changing and arbitrarily sculptured to create more sex 'criminals'.

With its attachment to children, and the disgusting thoughts that brings to mind, this list, and using it to encompass all sex-offenders, is a cheap, easy sale to a shallow, emotionally-based populous. And the fact it was used, outside of children, to encompass all sex-offenders suggests a pre-existing motive, accompanied by an occurrence that some thought could be used to get it through—an easy avenue to effect a dictatorship type of government control. This list of condemnation amounts to branding people, even after their sentences have been served. The Nazi-type procedure (and a protocol supporting it) has never before existed in our country nor has it been implemented upon our people which relentless persecution is a violation of our freedom and liberties, including rights to privacy. (Once the sentence has been served, the price is to be paid.) This same emotionally-based influence/exploitation attached to children was used pertaining to the Sandy Hook incident in an attempt to take away our gun rights and after the 9/11 attacks under President George Bush Jr. as an excuse to take away our rights to privacy which included sex-imposing laws pertaining to use of the Internet.

Child porn is now used, via emotions attached to the idea, as an avenue to persecute people, invade privacy, and threaten our freedom.

Child porn, especially its creation and using children to create it is a problem, of course, with the thought of associating children with sexual activity very repulsive. But that is also the ruse. There exists a Nazi mentality associated with seeking out those looking at and possessing child porn. And those who oppose this invasion into our private lives and abuse of our rights are automatically judged by others, possessing a shallow thinking capacity, to be child sex offenders themselves—how self-serving for the tyrants and bigots who support them. But in reality, this is all well-orchestrated 'emotional justice'. Politicians and law enforcement are cowards who in many cases merely prey on those who use porn, and in the process they exploit child victims of porn, or that is under-aged porn for their own gain at others' expense. Many examples are lumped together to be child porn even if those viewed are sexually-developed sixteen or seventeen year-olds. Also keep in mind that many people possess 'cute' baby pictures that now also qualify as child porn. A major distinction must be made here.

We also need to keep in mind that many who possess child porn are not the violators of these children, but they are easy to criminalize and catch—used by the authorities to represent the big catch when they are merely looking at a product of those who may have violated children. They haven't had physical contact, nor are they the ones who took the pictures or had any shared presence with them at all.

Let's be realistic. What harm are they doing? Is not more harm committed by someone who assaults someone? But these are children, some may respond. No, these are their images, and often they are not of little innocents but of young sexually-developed, under-aged youth who easily pass for young adults, not what comes to mind by using the term children and the emotions that stirs within.

Sure, some of these people may be messed up in their heads, unless an older under-aged teen poses (or whose image is used to pose) for one of legal age of consent. But even they are not harming anyone. In fact, it's best they are secluded in privacy where they can do no harm. (Is rounding up homosexuals next?)

A clue to illegitimacy we'll notice is that usually no actual harm is mentioned by these law enforcement officials who are merely looking for credos, and the people they target often have had no actual contact with the children in question. This merely amounts to the thought police. Indeed, more harm is done by an assault, with less jail time served for that (real harm) than for what a person looks at and may or may not be *thinking* regarding a mere image.

Indeed, have we now invaded people's minds and become the thought police? The public is being duped by the government and political manipulators through emotional appeal. This hype is based on what we think others are thinking and that they may be getting off on children, not about any harm they are actually doing. Sure, again, certain sexual thoughts are disgusting if applied to children, and that is the image/tool being used. But viewing imagery is still not committing any act that harms anyone, including children, and since when do we punish people for what they think or look at? We are using the emotional component as the clincher to determine guilt—not children but their imagery and what we think is going on in the minds of others, not their acts.

[However, a woman held in a position of public trust of children who not only has physical sexual contact but drugs and sexually assaults several children, gets off without even being deemed a sex offender or is required to register as a sex offender, spending merely two days in jail? Refer to Child sex charge dropped against former nurse at http://www.ktvb.com/news/crime/child-sex-charge-dropped-against-former-nurse/72093490. And this takes place in the same location where less than two years prior a man was sought out for possessing child porn in his home, arrested, and had to register as a sex offender, and sentenced to 6 1/2 years in prison!? Refer to Man gets 6.5 years for child porn at http://www.argusobserver.com/news/man-gets-years-for-child-porn/article_3da40c52-c006-11e3-bd0b-001a4bcf887a.html). This topic also relates to male suicide.]

In addition, many know they are not guilty of possessing what they (or the average person) considers child porn, and this is why they often willingly give law enforcement permission to access their computers, as is what occurred in the case cited above. But just like a cop planting a gun to 'justify' shooting a suspect, law enforcement will lace legitimate/legal porn with child porn to get a conviction. But again, what harm is actually being done by the one possessing the porn? It's all politically-driven.

Don't give the authorities permission to access your computer, even if you know you are innocent and are under pressure, via shame used to do it—e.g. "What have you got to hide if you are innocent?" The answer is: "My privacy, allowing me to be protected from government thugs like you and what you may arbitrarily interpret to be child porn," is an appropriate response. This threat to our freedom affects us all. One doesn't have to be personally involved to be affected as an American because the threat to our freedom affects (and is felt by) all Americans as a whole.

"A rguing that you don't care about the right to privacy because you have nothing to hide is no different than saying you don't care about free speech because you have nothing to say" (Edward Snowden). Refer to *In One Quote, Snowden Just Destroyed the Biggest Myth About Privacy* at https://mic.com/articles/119602/in-one-quote-edward-snowden-summed-up-why-our-privacy-is-worth-fighting-for#.8NSazICsc.

Something that is not illegal, but is not considered acceptable by a certain segment of the population, is being used to target and criminalize a segment of our population through an invasion of their privacy via the emotional use of children. What better way exists to get the support of Conservatives (who hypocritically boast of their opposition to government intrusion) on the side of government to take away our freedom than to tap into their minds by using porn and the emotional effects of children being violated to do it? See it for what it actually is—government Nazi techniques embraced through emotional appeal. Also refer to "If You Don't Have Anything To Hide, You Shouldn't Care About NSA Spying" DEBUNKED at https://www.youtube.com/watch?v=CG8hIcc7b80.

[Note: As for the sacrifice of our rights and freedom, it matters not whether it be through liberal or conservative means. Merely the issues held by either camp determine what rights are sacrificed or retained.]

Many people are afraid to say anything against this government intrusion because they are held by fear of being labeled child sex offenders themselves if they do. This works out very well for law enforcement thugs and government tyrants. Those possessing real courage will stand up to these invasive Gestopo-type people, laws, and law enforcement practices. As sheep falling in line, it doesn't take any courage to jump on this emotionally-charged bandwagon, and doing so only feeds the problem—that of tyranny now affecting all aspects of our society.

And women/mothers, who many men and law enforcement strive to please, are often the most effective implementing this type of child-related emotional influence. Here again we have a prime example of what can be termed "emotional intelligence" often bound by a chivalry component.

When you smell a rat, you know it's there, you just have to flush it out. There is federal money attached to this persecution by law enforcement, and as money now commonly buys off our rights and those agencies entrusted to protect them, local law enforcement receives federal money to fund this persecution. A state that works too closely with the feds to receive this funding is suspect. (The same is evident in federal funds received for domestic violence, child support collection, and social services, including child 'protection'.)

Just like sex, porn is not illegal, but under-aged sex or porn is illegal. However, child porn is subjective, not only because it is mere electronic imagery, but because the law does not differentiate by appearance between a 'child' of seventeen, who easily passes as a legal adult (and may be legal in some states), and an adult over 18. Nor does it distinguish in violation degree categorization between small children and those who are sexually-developed passing as legal adults that would allow a discrepancy due to appearance between what is legal and what is a felony. It's an easy set-up, and one that only applies to imagery. Due to the fact one is not in the presence of the other person to hold that person accountable by identification, the image is all that exists to convey a legal age of consent. And a consent to what, merely look?

Shouldn't people be free to look at whatever they want, anyway, and to do so within the privacy of their homes? These are people who in their acts are confined to their computers and pose no threat to anyone. Regardless of the self-serving reason, this intrusive, emotionally-derived law enforcement is an invasion of people's freedom and their privacy. The people convicted are branded for life as sex offenders; their gun rights are also taken away (when no weapon, let alone gun, is involved); they can't live near a park or a school, and must register as sex offenders. We should not tolerate this crap. It never existed in our past. Placed within the context of all the other efforts this serves by the government as another effective means to take over and control the people, especially with the endorsement of the people through their emotions and fear to oppose. We must have some immunity in the privacy of our own homes.

Just like the discrimination violations by the VAWA, privacy violations through the government seeking child porn provides another avenue ('excuse') to violate our Constitutional rights, enabling the government, with the help of the police and the public (informants), to no longer help protect our rights but to assist in taking them away.

The subjective nature determining child porn is a direct threat to our freedom, the definition including what have in the past been considered cute baby pictures, National Geographic documentaries or old movies (e.g. Lord of the Flies) one may have in his or her possession that show naked children. In the course of educating her daughter about her sexuality, one mother took photos of her daughter's privates so her daughter could look at them. As many of us can recall, women libbers used mirrors in their conveyances of female self-discovery to do the same. Upon discovery of these photos through a government informant (what appeared to be her daughter's girlfriend's mother), this girl's mother was charged with possessing child porn. The pictures were confiscated and the daughter was taken into custody by state authorities. Although the mother and father were separated, the child's father defended the mother. Was it really worth it? Did this not do more damage to the child than the mother did by taking the pictures? These Nazi techniques and laws are only accepted by a stupid people who allow emotions to over-ride logical thought processes, the same as preceded the Holocaust. Refer to Mom accused of selling nude pictures of daughter at http://www.good4utah.com/contact/marcos-ortiz/mom-accused-of-selling-nude-pictures-of-daughter.

Hypocrisy disclosed by practice:

A complete revelation of lunacy practiced by our government per child porn law is openly revealed in the following case when an individual is held accountable as an adult and as a child at the same time—charged in a child porn case for possessing pictures of *himself*. Refer to Teen boy charged as adult for having 'naked pictures of a minor' even though images were of himself at http://www.countercurrentnews.com/2015/09/teen-boy-charged-as-adult. How subjective and hypocritical it is that he is only 17 and the authorities are charging him as an adult? As the article questions, ""how can a teen be old enough to face adult, felony charges, but not old enough to keep a nude picture of himself on his phone?"" If he is an adult then there is nothing illegal about having a nude photo of himself. However, the time-travel 'justice' effect could then be applied if the photos were taken when he was 17. It's ridiculous. However, this case brings to light the illegitimate stand of child porn. The law is like some computer glitch in which case it can't function correctly due to lack of reasoning capability. (A legitimate law is sound, not emotionally-based or destroyed by reason.) This boy, a high school quarterback, is now a felony sex offender, but of who, himself? He is therefore committing a crime every time he looks at himself, bathes, or goes to the bathroom! This completely exposes the problem with mere photos/electronic images being a crime in itself—they are not real people but images, and with no age designation. The authorities have created a false and unsubstantiated entity that has been used to form an unfounded precedence, needlessly convicting real people when no crime is committed against a person by the 'offender'. The connection to a person or any violation is lost, replaced by an obsession with mere possession of *an image* as being the violation. Thus, as in this case, the "evidence" is himself but how can he violate himself by his own birthday suit? This demonstrates that pictures alone mean nothing as evidence and constitute no violation of anyone by the one possessing them. A point brought to light here made earlier is: What distinguishes by imagery the difference between a boy or girl under 18 and one over 18? And are we using time travel to create the violation? The same boy of 17 is now 18— legal. And no other person even exists in this case. An entity has been created outside of reality (deemed an unlawful sex act without any tangible/person connection) for arbitrary persecution purposes. Did the 17-year-old high school quarterback have sex with himself? Again, what harm is done?

Media, Politics, and Educational Bias

All politics, laws, education and informational services must express a lack of sex-bias to be considered legitimate. Sex-based preference in politics, media and education is to be illegal and an expression of sex-bigotry (misandry) so common now against men.

Disallow any law that discriminates on the basis of sex:

Violence against anyone is to be an equal concern regardless of sex or gender. Disallow any law that discriminates on the basis of sex—e.g. VAWA, Title IX. This is also unconstitutional, and laws that are so are illegal and have to standing. Our U.S. Constitution must always be upheld for our country to remain in tact.

Hold women to an equal level of Sexual Accountability to men, socially and legally

When a woman brings sexual attention to herself and a man is present, unless she is sincere, this is her sexual violation of him. And she is responsible for the sex act this may summon as a result. Common sense sex laws of the past were based on this premise.

When a man in prison doesn't want sex does he ask for it (solicit it) and try to visually stimulate other men? Of course not. Thus the same accountability standard must apply to women and their inter-relations with men. Women's lingerie and porn are both products of this well-known fact of male visual stimulation. As in the past the same sexual summoning was kept to the bedroom. As the sex act is being instigated on a woman's behalf, she assumes an obligation to follow through just as competent laws were sculptured in the past to equally take men into consideration.

There comes a point when a man commits himself (as a matter of trust) as he submits/succumbs to a woman's sexual influence when "Yes" is conveyed by her just as when a woman (although not as intense as a need) is physically stimulated by a man—a temporary contract of sexual obligation/trust occurs. (Even animals have this basic understanding.) Otherwise, the female's conveyance is only another form of dishonesty. The means (visual versus physical) is different but the sex act is often initiated by the female per her visual stimulation of the male—a well-known means used per lingerie and porn, often accompanied by suggestive sexual posture, behavior, gestures and verbal expression.

Some calloused individuals say in support of the female's (often deliberate) violation of males and ill-intentions, that men need to practice "self-control" when they are the ones being teased/violated by women. But from the male's perspective, this is no different than saying a woman needs to therefore practice self-control and not be bothered if the sex act is 'against her will'. This sexual abuse initiated on the female's behalf is against his will!

The idea of sex not being acceptable/permissible is only applied against the male's sexuality and his sexual response, not against the expression of the female's sexuality and to what is often her initiation of the act. She is to have the same restrictions placed on the expression of her sexuality as is placed on the expression of the male's sexuality, or restrictions applying to the male's sexual expression lifted. Unless an equal restriction is to exist, what's termed self-control is not to be an issue/applicable 'excuse' under conditions that are already set within the perimeters of mutual sexual participation between two adults. When the sex act is initiated by the female, the male, under an equal standing to the female, reacting in kind, has no reason to restrain himself (practice "self-control"—the female isn't doing so), since sex— what she is offering—is something he seeks to have, and she knows it. Only by exonerating female accountability is the male held more liable in the situation, with his perspective not included or considered in the matter. When a man is not only ridiculed but criminalized for his sexual response to a woman (performing his normal role), a natural part of his personal and basic biological existence is violated, and this is not right nor healthy for anyone, with a man's equal rights violated as a human being of supposed equal status.

What adds to the injustice due to the male's dirty/guilty sexual stigma is his violation is often portrayed as 'humorus' as if he somehow 'deserves' to be deprived and punished for his needs ('naughty desires'). This emphasizes women's 'innocent' stand, although they are the dishonest culprets.

The female is no innocent who initiates the sex act through her visual stimulation of a man (again, women's lingerie and porn, purposely created for men's visual means of sexual stimulation, are all proof of this), and when in person the effect is immensely intensified by anxiety in anticipation of potential sexual fulfilment and from one who should be trusted in the normal course of a sexual encounter—and thus by a supposed adult equal of mutual social responsibility and maturity to a man. Due to the female's sexual effects, a man is dominated by a woman, yet she is not held accountable for her dominance—an extreme abuse of female power through which men are subjectively criminalized.

[Note: Women knowingly convey their sexual effects then hypocritically complain about men responding to them, purposely defying that men are sexually stimulated through visual means. And thereafter they even have the gall to say women aren't here to meet a man's needs. Really? Then they shouldn't act like they are or get off on the deceitful effects representing that they are.]

Legitimate claims of rape by men exist in prison because men in prison are held to accountability that women are not. Men do not ask for sex amongst men as women do unless they expect to provide it to them, so why would this same level of accountability (ethical principle) not equally apply to women as used to be the case when rape (whether the criminal act per law occurred or not) was determined by what the female is wearing and her manner of behaviour? Men in prison are forced into homosexual sex *without* provocation! Would a man who *'asks for it'* amongst men be considered innocent and a victim as are women who do the same with men? Of course not.

An unspoken commitment to completing the sex act was realized in the past by both parties (men and women) as responsible adults. Females of other animal species express the same to convey their consent. Is the human female now less responsible for her actions than females of other species? Must a sexual consent contract be available on the spot. (But would that only apply to female terms and thus after the male has been teased/violated?) Due to patronizing modern female incompetence, would the law even honor something that holds modern-day women to an equal accountability level to men?

It appears that by their own hand women are not only digressing back to (but defending) a time when women weren't considered capable of doing many things that males were capable of, now even digressing below an adult female status they held in the past concerning basic social/sexual interactions. And this social incompetence even applies to an exclusive power they possess. Yet, this lack of social/sexual competence is being patronised and compensated. Women have lowered themselves to the status of children and minors, not as consenting adults of equal competence and accountability to men. This discrepancy and discriminatory effect must be abolished for standards of equal justice and equality of the sexes to exist.

Reckless and irresponsible sexual behavior is not to be patronized by sex-biased laws that allow women to decieve, violate, and criminalize men. So extreme is this that men are now even held accountable for women and the choices they make and conditions that apply to both, as if either party is intoxicated deeming it rape of only by the male. Both, consuming alcohol and sex, are not illegal. This is now applying. per law, a woman's status as a child rather than as an equal to a man. This is openly discriminatory. And men are now charged for indulging in prostitution when all that makes sex between two consenting adults illegal is that *the woman charges*.

Men's equality must retain its Male integrity to be Effective

Some MRAs treat women as authorities in the men's equality effort. Why? Do they need women's approval? Women who are MRAs are to be respected and appreciated, but they are not to be regarded as authorities (above men) in the cause. Are men placed as authorities in women's organizations? No. We don't find men as prominent figures in women's organizations Men need to first come to terms as MRAs and oppose other men before they can proceed and compromise with women to produce any legitimate equal-termed results. Women who fight for men's rights, although honorable, can not begin to understand or appreciate the full scope of men's equal rights to women and often express ulterior motives, merely wanting something back (e.g. a male yoke of servitude from the past) they lost—still a female bias. How many women are willing to give up their privileges (not rights, for these are at the expense and exclusion of men) for men? At best their leadership involvement will limit the full scope of men's rights.

The fact there are women placed as prominent figures in men's organizations is apparently due to an a male insecurity as to how males have been groomed from boyhood to only feel legitimized if they receive female approval. Thus the very influence men need to overcome acquiring an equal status to women is preventing them from getting it. [And good luck trying to get such a study funded—one that determines the extent of the female-groomed influence.] Yet nothing, no compromise due to any blind devotion to men, governs women's expression. Although there are many chivalrous male followers, men are not allowed to represent women.

Equal Funding for Education, opportunities, research, and exclusive Issues or tainted record-keeping in securing references

Return unbiased integrity to references, education, and research, to include better filters with no biases catering to women and female politics. No funding is to be appropriated to women over men in programs for education, cancer research, or any other entity unless equally appropriated to men. No funding is to be robbed attributed to men for women either. (e.g. Tile IX took resources from men who created it and outnumbered women). Sports originated from men and so did the funding appropriated to it per proven athleticism derived and evolving through men. Men were already more sports oriented by nature, and the allocation of money generated by them proves to be directly correlated with more male athletes involved toward whom those funds should be appropriated.

School programs are to also recognize the differences between boys and girls and sculpture their teaching methods accordingly—accommodating these recognized sex-differences in education rather than coercing boys into oppressive conformity to a female-based standard.

Homosexuality

Homosexuality is a neutral issue concerning men's equality except that male homosexuality is to be considered equally acceptable to female homosexuality. As the male's sexuality is deemed dirty and less acceptable to the female's sexuality, the effect is further enhanced through male homosexuality. This is where men's rights include gay rights. Both male and female forms of homosexuality are to be regarded with equal acceptance. But this doesn't mean that homosexuality is to be accepted as some form of standard. Nor should it be allowed to invade and threaten heterosexual activities either. [e.g. No invasiveness is to be tolerated. Just like Special Teams, transgenders should be relegated to their own sports teams and not allowed to participate in games due to the gender they identify as. The same principle also applies to women to not be allowed to invade male sports as football. This includes authoritative announcers and referees of the male exclusive sport. Retain the integrity of the sport to which the sex playing it applies.]

Homosexuality is not normal per nature. Genetics are only passed through heterosexuality. Basically all but 2.5% results from an environmental influence, and we have seen that occur by the masses via a political coercive influence. Reference books of psychology used to recognize homosexuality as abnormal, but only due to politics was that changed in reference in the 1970s. Although homosexuality is not to be accepted as the standard, every individual is to have equal rights regardless of their gender preference or identity. Neither male or female homosexuals, or those in between, are to be rated any different or more acceptable—e.g. lesbians or gays—to each other nor to heterosexuals and be granted more rights than heterosexuals. We at Newsofx.com stand against bigotry toward homosexuals.

Equal Personal Worth and Value is to be Granted to Men:

Newsofx.com advocates equal personal worth and value be provided to men and maintains that men's intimacy and privacy is to be equally regarded and honored to women's. [Women reporters have been allowed to violate men's sexual privacy by entering men's locker rooms. Less than less is a sexual violation of women. This is to be deemed a sex crime against men committed by women.]

Further built upon the disregard of the male's intimacy and its degraded status, is the lack of its value compared to women's. This is further evident from the 'humor' received from its abuse or destruction and heinious acts as the Lorena Bobbit incident. What used to be referred to as a man's family jewels are now his junk. This constrasts with a woman's sexual body parts. They are fully appreciated and highly regarded.

Concepts covered here are from Alan Millard and his book [*A Flaw From Within*].

The Indian Chapter of Newsofx.com

In India there is a saying "Mard Ko Dard Nahi Hota Hai" which means men don't feel the pain. This calloused expression reveals the disregard appropriated to men and alerts us to how men are the deliberate recipients of injustice. Men are not to be stereotyped as criminals or categorized as personally inferior and conveniently deemed disposable for others of a 'superior' status (women). There are more than 50 Indian laws favoring women, and this creates more male criminals.

A Men's Commission

An independent ministry for women and children called the "Ministry of Women & Children" has existed for many years. There are additional plans and policies for girls and women by the government to include stipend, reservations and priority programs for women's education in schools/colleges. Both the Central Government and State governments have a women's commission. (The Constitution of India establishes a federal structure, declaring India to be a "Union of States." Part XI of the Indian constitution specifies the distribution of legislative, administrative, and executive powers between the Union/Federal/Central Government and the States of India.) This structure promotes enhanced women's rights with negligible checks and balances. This is discriminatory as men are subjected to almost no support, enhanced abuse and injustice (by various government machinery) as compared to women. The law against false cases is very weak and does not allow any compensation or legal support from the government. For example, if a woman accuses a man of sexually exploiting her, the man is immediately arrested and the state fights the case on behalf of the woman. If after many years the man is able to prove his innocence then after complete satisfaction the court will exonerate the man and only record an observation that the woman eccentric laws, meant to protect women, are being increasingly misused. So the courts will give an option to the man who was accused till now, to file a separate case of defamation against the woman. However, hypocrically expressing discriminatory practice, the state will not fight the case against women. And there is no law to immediately punish the woman upon conclusion of the first case, although the innocent man was punished. In many cases women don't even turn up to fight the case or record their statement and later it is realized the case was filed just to settle personal score against the man and his family. And this blatant misuse goes unabated. Even Bangladesh, a country with a small Hindu population has stringent laws to punish women abusing dowry laws which were meant to protect them. This sex discrimination is not to be tolerated. Men are to receive no less than equal protection to women.

The Indian government does not allocate any funding in its annual budget for men's rights/issues. The misuse of these women eccentric laws which allow false accusations include the Dowry Prohibition Act (498A), Domestic Violence, Misdeed or Rape / Sexual assault, Harassment in workplace, Protection of children from sexual offences. Any type of sex-discriminatory law against women, as for example the payment of dowry, has long been prohibited under specific Indian laws, including the 1961 Dowry Prohibition Act and subsequently by Sections 304B and 498A of the Indian Penal Code. There are many "me too" claims without any evidence or proof or substantiation. Often only providing a man's name to the authorities makes him a criminal. Even anonymous complaints are often considered valid and prosecuted.

Stringent Punishment for All False Accusers

Anyone, whether husband or wife, if guilty, should be punished. However, we find that because of female bias and discriminatory laws many innocent people are in jail. Many times the people in jail are found innocent after several years of incarceration. The incarceration of several years leads to job loss, severe financial crisis as they have to hire lawyers to fight the case; their families face severe hardship and trauma where they are declared guilty on the basis of a media trial, etc.

There should be stringent punishment for all false accusers—whether men or women. The person who gives false testimony needs to be punished in the same manner as the one who is convicted. There are many cases where a wife has accused her husband, his mother, sisters and grandmother who too are sent to a jail resulting in many innocent women in jail! Even hearsay from the family of the wife is enough for police to arrest the husband and his family including the distant relatives. Till some time ago it was not unusual to find a minor as young as 2 years be mentioned as an accused for domestic violence etc. Many sex-discriminatory laws like the dowry act 498A or rape laws support criminals who demand exorbitant money to take back their false allegations, often in connivance with police. This extortion is endorsed by government that acts as an accomplice patronising and endorsing these budding criminals. There are women who have filed multiple rape cases against multiple men in various courts and there is no way to check this menace.

Clearly there are discriminatory laws against men with a dire need for gender neutral laws. A proper investigation should be done with evidence documented. In India where women, children, animals, and forests have different commissions, should men not have one commission that would regulate their rights? Although Indian men exercise their voting rights, they have become second class citizens. In 2015 across India, 133,623 suicides were reported, of which 91,528 (68%) were by men, 42,088 were by women, according to data from National Crime Records Bureau (NCRB). Credit: NCRB, 2015 which suggests that one man commits suicide every 9 minutes. Amongst women, housewives (22,293) accounted for 53% of the total female victims whereas of all the men who committed suicide – 23% were daily wage earners (20,409) followed by persons engaged in farming sector (11,584) and self-employed persons (11,124). Amongst the 86,808 married persons who committed suicides in 2015, 64,534 (74%) were men, 26% women. However, of 28,344 suicides by married women, housewives accounted for 79% of them.

Men's integrity, to include their word, is to be given equal value to women's which only comes from men's equal status rather than a second-class status to women. Often evidence provided by an accused man or his family is not accepted, but if the woman just speaks out against him, a man is branded as a criminal. Many men are poor, sick, unemployed, and have to support a family, including elderly parents. Newsofx.com stresses the need to create a male welfare ministry. Poor men who cannot afford legal counsel should be provided with a legal counsel by the government. Gender neutral laws must be instated that provide equal justice to all. All political parties eying male votes must put down in their manifesto what they will do for men and pledge to create a national men's commission.

https://newsofx.com/about-us/

Newsofx.com, based out of India, writes on men's issues in India as well as all over the world.

Our Mission

Newsofx is about uniting Mens' Rights Activists and Mens' Rights groups and focusing on our common goal for men to gain equal rights to women. We incorporate information and knowledge from other men's rights groups and rationally define our path and follow it together. Today many men's rights groups are divided due to men being groomed from boyhood to serve women as part of their defined 'manhood'. They are their own worst enemies and enemies to other men who want to achieve an equal status to women. Newsofx.com represents a genuine men's equality effort in which case men are to be defined in their own right, not women's. This manifesto focuses on fighting female bias as chivalry, feminism, and general sex-bigotry against men (misandry), which applies to parent alienation, circumcision, gender biased laws, reproductive rights, domestic violence, and a degraded social status amongst many other facets of society.

9 781699 519950